AF599461

NFL ★ TEAM PROFILES

THE CAROLINA PANTHERS

BY THOMAS K. ADAMSON

EPIC

BELLWETHER MEDIA ★ MINNEAPOLIS, MN

EPIC BOOKS are no ordinary books. They burst with intense action, high-speed heroics, and shadows of the unknown. Are you ready for an Epic adventure?

This edition first published in 2024 by Bellwether Media, Inc.

Library of Congress Cataloging-in-Publication Data

Names: Adamson, Thomas K., 1970- author.
Title: The Carolina Panthers / by Thomas K. Adamson.
Description: Minneapolis, MN : Bellwether Media, 2024. | Series: Epic. NFL team profiles | Includes bibliographical references and index. | Audience: Ages 7-12 | Audience: Grades 2-3 | Summary: "Engaging images accompany information about the Carolina Panthers. The combination of high-interest subject matter and light text is intended for students in grades 2 through 7" -- Provided by publisher.
Identifiers: LCCN 2023021295 (print) | LCCN 2023021296 (ebook) | ISBN 9798886874709 (library binding) | ISBN 9798886876581 (ebook)
Subjects: LCSH: Carolina Panthers (Football team)--History--Juvenile literature.
Classification: LCC GV956.C27 A33 2024 (print) | LCC GV956.C27 (ebook) | DDC 796.332/640975676--dc23/eng/20230511
LC record available at https://lccn.loc.gov/2023021295
LC ebook record available at https://lccn.loc.gov/2023021296

Editor: Elizabeth Neuenfeldt   Designer: Gabriel Hilger

Printed in the United States of America, North Mankato, MN.

TABLE OF CONTENTS

NFC CHAMPIONS!

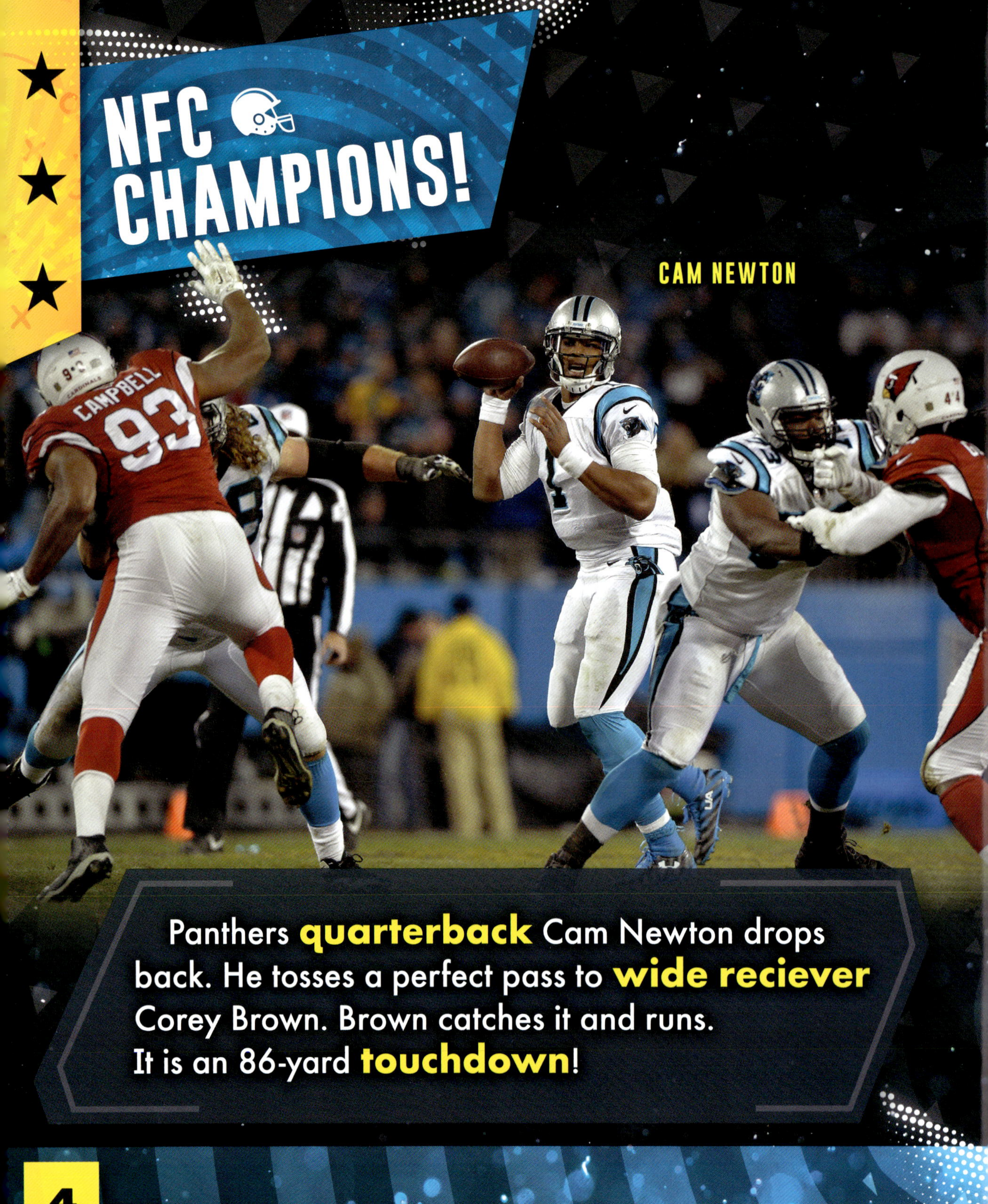

CAM NEWTON

Panthers **quarterback** Cam Newton drops back. He tosses a perfect pass to **wide reciever** Corey Brown. Brown catches it and runs. It is an 86-yard **touchdown**!

The Panthers go on to win. They advance to their second **Super Bowl**!

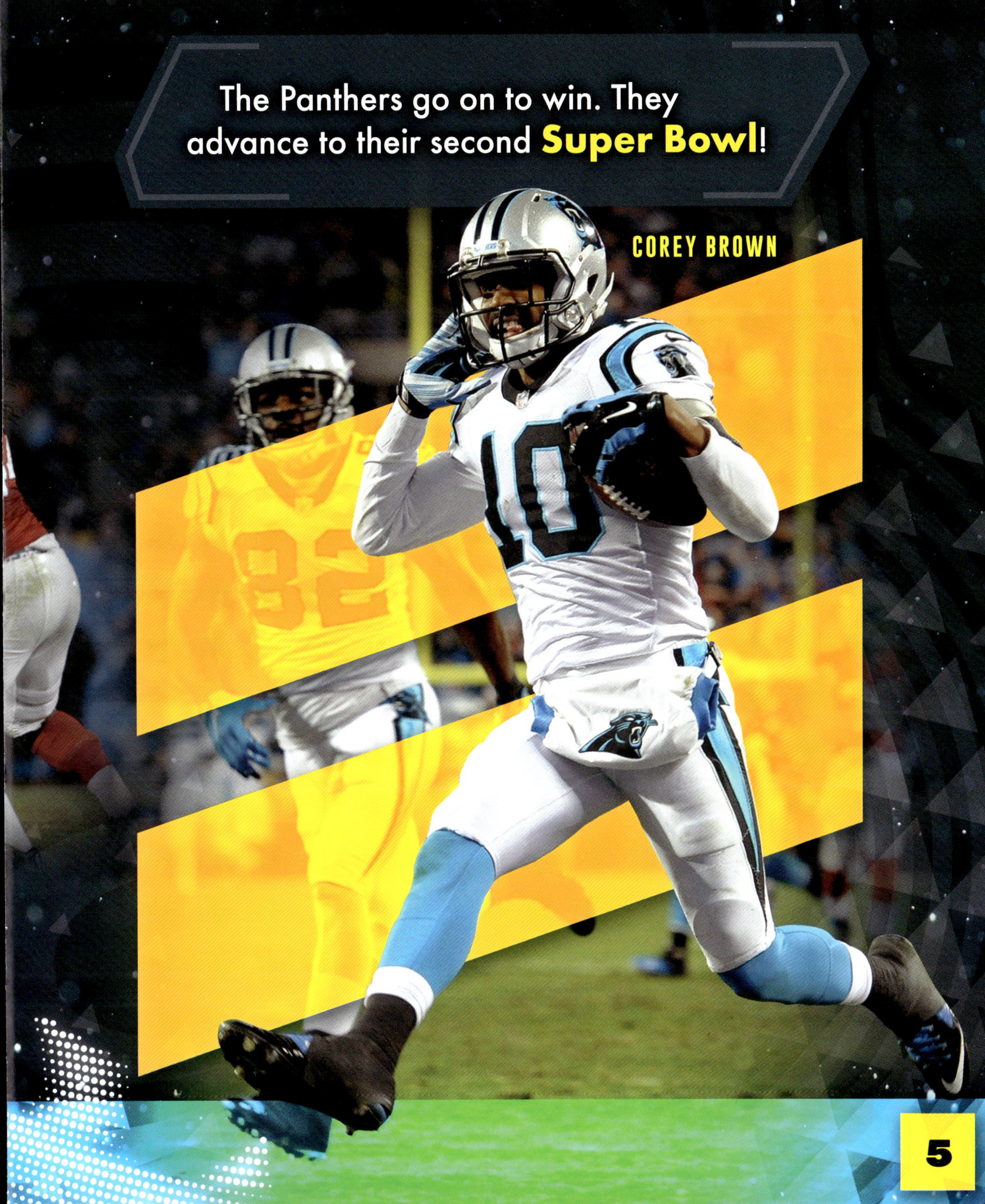

THE HISTORY OF THE PANTHERS

The National Football League (NFL) added new teams in 1993. Fans in North and South Carolina wanted a team. They showed support to get one.

The team was called the Panthers. They were based in Charlotte, North Carolina. They began playing in 1995.

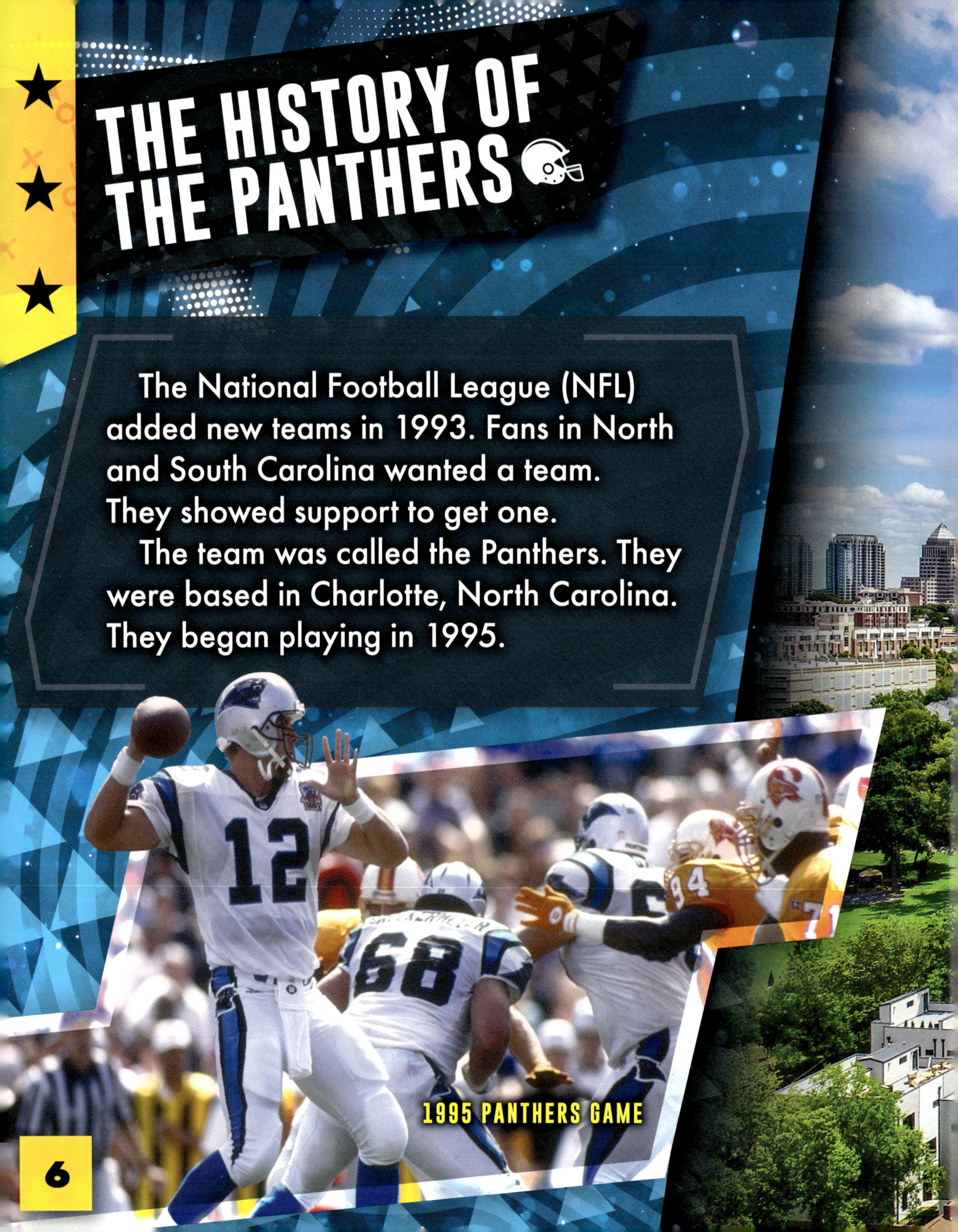

1995 PANTHERS GAME

THE NFL GROWS

The Panthers and the Jacksonville Jaguars were the first new NFL teams since 1976.

The Panthers played well in their first season. They won 7 games in 1995.

1995 PANTHERS GAME

FAST START

The Panthers' first season set an NFL record. They had the most wins for a new team!

1996 NFC CHAMPIONSHIP GAME

The Panthers won 12 games in their second season. They reached the NFC **Championship** Game. But they lost.

The Panthers' early success did not last long. They had several losing seasons.

2002 PANTHERS GAME

In 2001, wide receiver Steve Smith joined the team. He helped the Panthers reach Super Bowl 38 in 2004! But they lost to the New England Patriots.

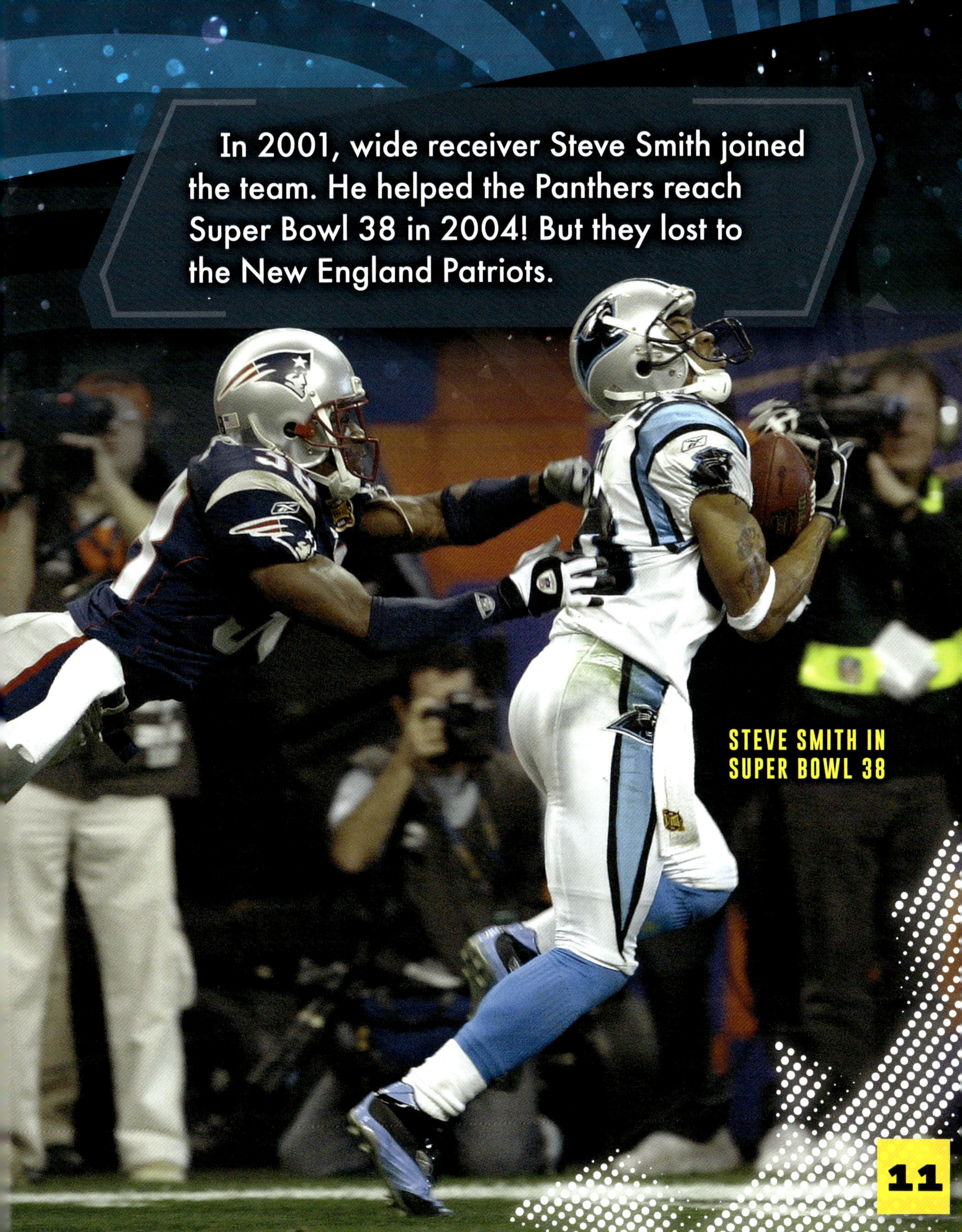

STEVE SMITH IN SUPER BOWL 38

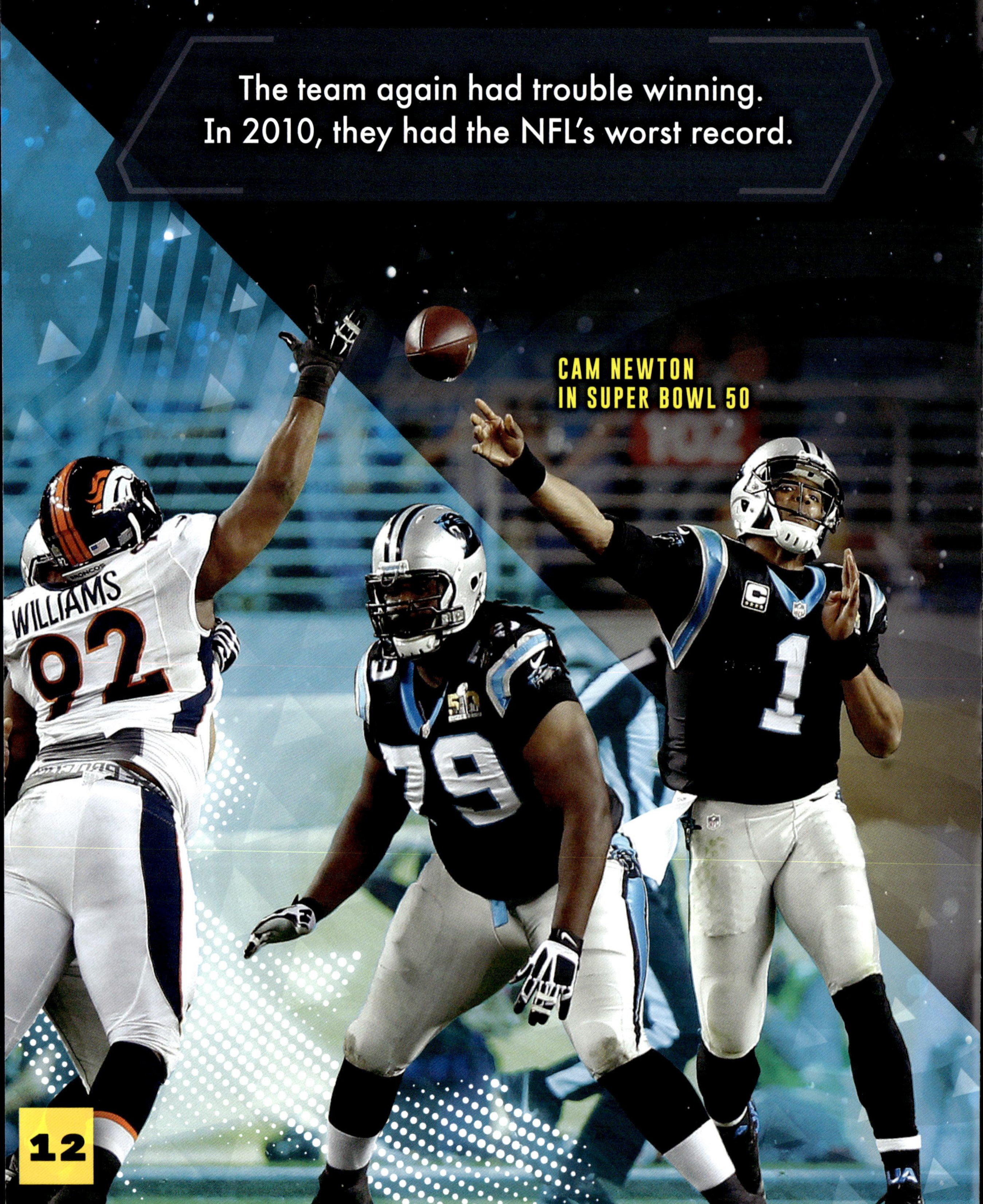

The team again had trouble winning. In 2010, they had the NFL's worst record.

CAM NEWTON
IN SUPER BOWL 50

That allowed them to **draft** Cam Newton. In 2016, he led the team to their second Super Bowl. But they lost to the Denver Broncos.

THE PANTHERS TODAY

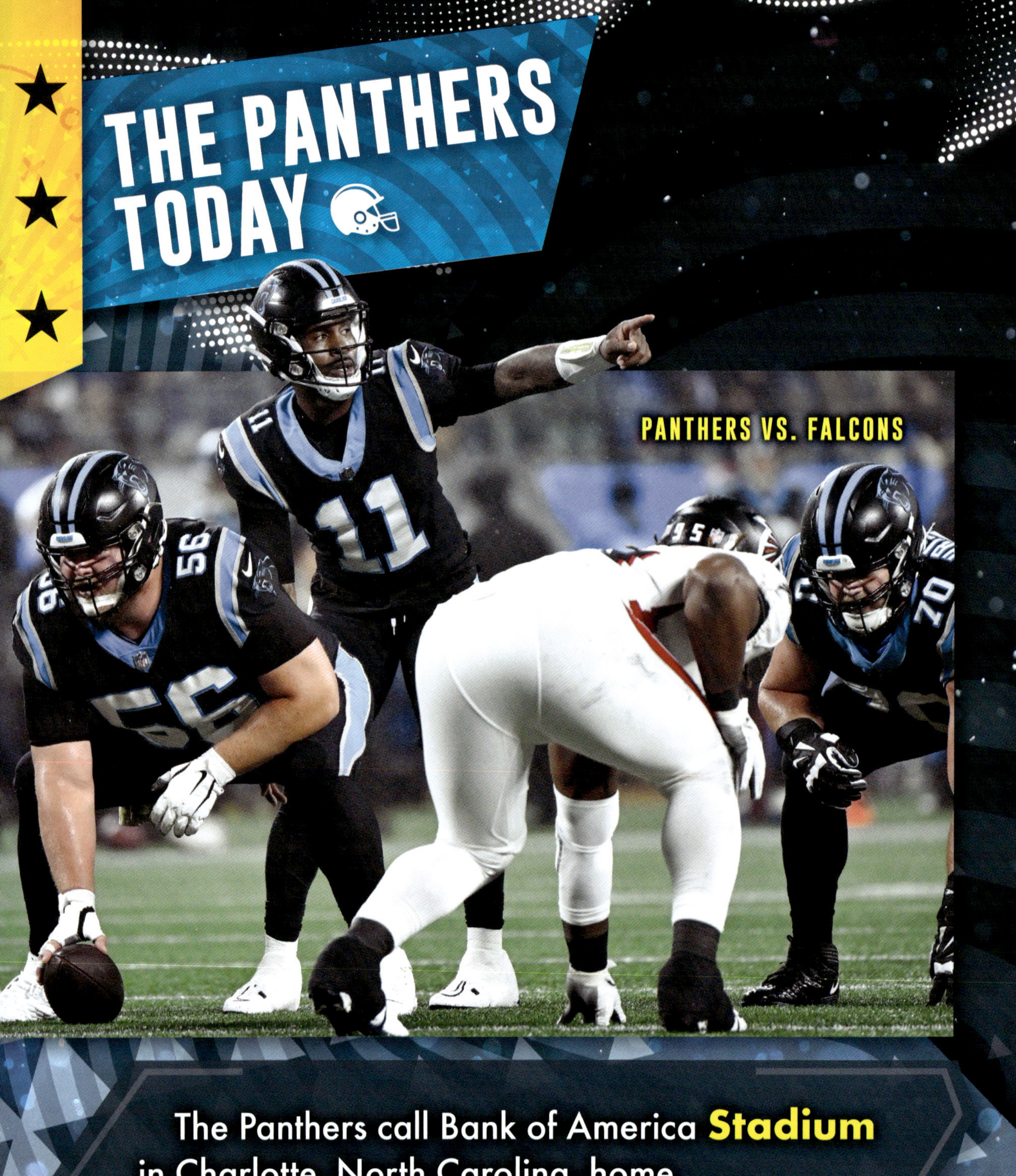

PANTHERS VS. FALCONS

The Panthers call Bank of America **Stadium** in Charlotte, North Carolina, home.

The team plays in the NFC South **division**. Their biggest **rival** is the Atlanta Falcons.

SAME SUPER BOWL OPPONENTS

The Panthers and Falcons have both lost two Super Bowls. Both teams lost to the Broncos and the Patriots.

LOCATION

BANK OF AMERICA STADIUM

Charlotte, North Carolina

GAME DAY!

The Panthers' **mascot** is Sir Purr. He gets fans to cheer!

Before home games, a video shows a giant panther pouncing across the scoreboard. It grabs the opposing team's flag. Then the panther tears the flag.

SIR PURR

Game day sounds get fans cheering at home games. A wild cat growl signals a Panthers **first down**.

The PurrCussion **drumline** gets fans pumped up. After a win, fans sing "Sweet Caroline" to honor their team!

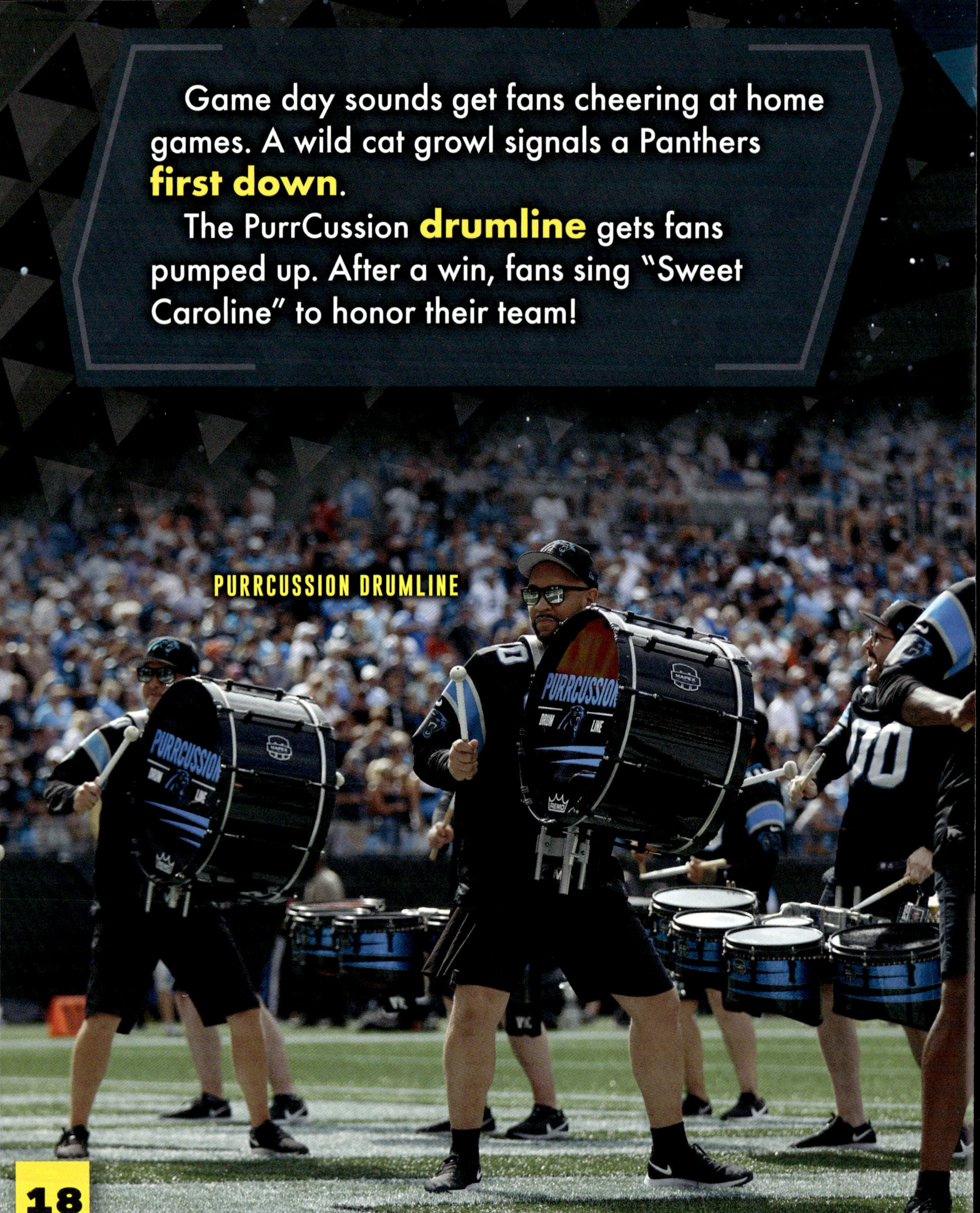

PURRCUSSION DRUMLINE

★ FAMOUS PLAYERS ★

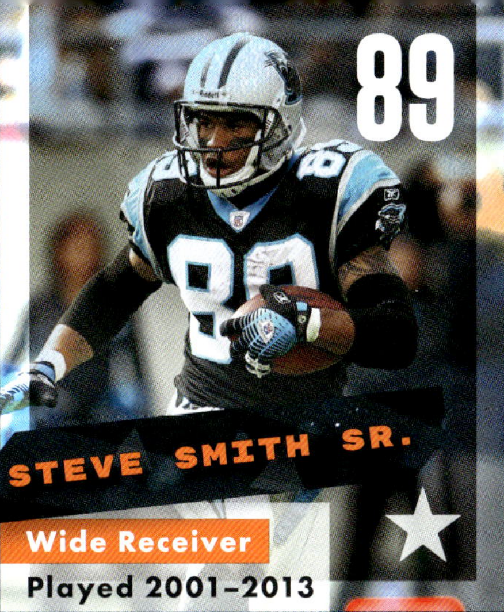

STEVE SMITH SR.

Wide Receiver

Played 2001–2013

CAM NEWTON

Quarterback

Played 2011–2019, 2021

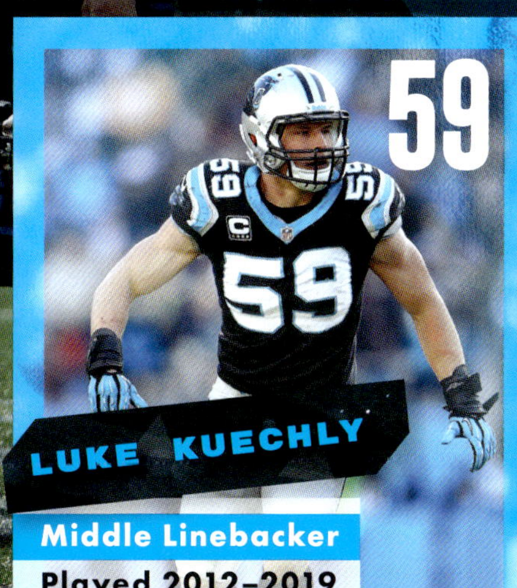

LUKE KUECHLY

Middle Linebacker

Played 2012–2019

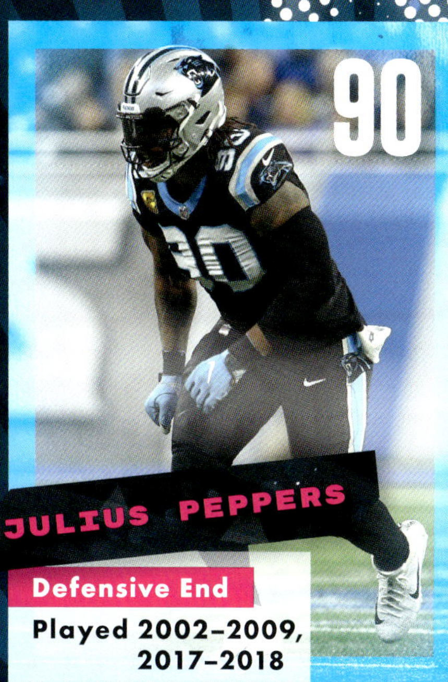

JULIUS PEPPERS

Defensive End

Played 2002–2009, 2017–2018

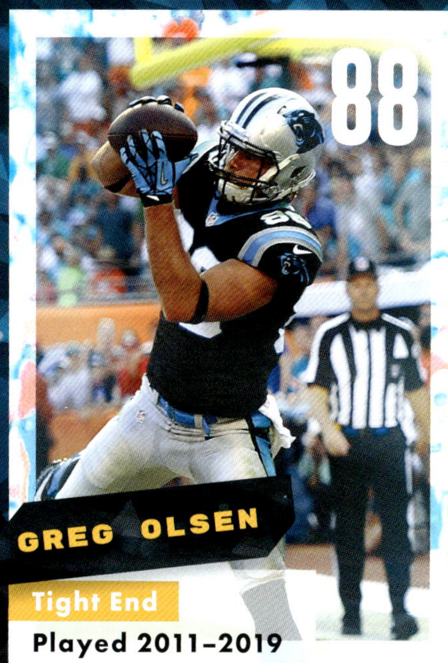

GREG OLSEN

Tight End

Played 2011–2019

CAROLINA PANTHERS FACTS

LOGO

JOINED THE NFL	1995
NICKNAME	Cardiac Cats

MASCOT

CONFERENCE

National Football Conference (NFC)

COLORS

DIVISION | NFC South

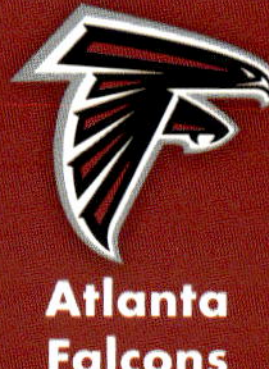
Atlanta Falcons

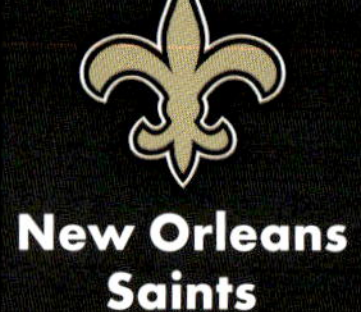
New Orleans Saints

Tampa Bay Buccaneers

STADIUM

★ BANK OF AMERICA STADIUM ★

opened September 14, 1996

holds 74,867 people

TIMELINE

1993
The NFL adds the Panthers as a new team from North Carolina

1995
The Panthers win their first game

2004
The Panthers lose Super Bowl 38

2011
The Panthers draft Cam Newton

2016
The Panthers lose Super Bowl 50

RECORDS

All-Time Receiving Leader
Steve Smith Sr.
12,197 yards

All-Time Rushing Leader
Jonathan Stewart
7,318 yards

All-Time Passing Leader
Cam Newton
29,725 yards

Single-Season Passing Leader
Steve Beuerlein
4,436 yards in 1999

GLOSSARY

championship—a contest to decide the best team or person

division—a group of NFL teams from the same area that often play against each other; there are eight divisions in the NFL.

draft—to choose a college athlete to play for a professional team

drumline—a group of musicians who play drums and cymbals, usually to pump up a crowd

first down—when a football team gets a new set of downs after gaining at least 10 yards; teams get four downs to gain 10 yards.

mascot—an animal or symbol that represents a sports team

quarterback—a player whose main job is to throw and hand off the ball

rival—a long-standing opponent

stadium—an arena where sports are played

Super Bowl—the annual championship game of the NFL

touchdown—a score that occurs when a team crosses into their opponent's end zone with the football; a touchdown is worth six points.

wide receiver—a player whose main job is to catch passes from the quarterback

TO LEARN MORE

AT THE LIBRARY

Abdo, Kenny. *Carolina Panthers.* Minneapolis, Minn.: Abdo Zoom, 2022.

Coleman, Ted. *Carolina Panthers: All-time Greats.* Mendota Heights, Minn.: Press Room Editions, 2022.

Whiting, Jim. *The Story of the Carolina Panthers.* Minneapolis, Minn.: Kaleidoscope, 2020.

ON THE WEB

FACTSURFER

Factsurfer.com gives you a safe, fun way to find more information.

1. Go to www.factsurfer.com.
2. Enter "Carolina Panthers" into the search box and click 🔍.
3. Select your book cover to see a list of related content.

INDEX

The images in this book are reproduced through the courtesy of: Brian Westerholt/ AP Images, cover, pp. 18-19; CLS Digital Arts, cover (stadium); Jacob Kupferman/ Stringer/ Getty, p. 3; Grant Halverson/ Stringer, pp. 4, 14, 21 (Steve Smith Sr., Jonathan Stewart); Jared C. Tilton/ Stringer, p. 5; Jamie Squire/ Staff/ Getty, p. 6; Kevin Ruck, pp. 6-7; Focus On Sport/ Contributor/ Getty, pp. 8, 21 (Steve Beuerlein); David Stluka/ AP Images, p. 9; Tom Pidgeon/ Stringer/ Getty, p. 10; Brian Bahr/ Staff/ Getty, pp. 10-11; Ezra Shaw/ Staff/ Getty, p. 12; Grindstone Media Group, p. 15 (Band of America Stadium); NFL/ Wikipedia, pp. 15 (Carolina Panthers logo), 19 (Atlanta Falcons logo, Carolina Panthers logo, New Orleans Saints logo, Tampa Bay Buccaneers logo, NFC logo); Stephen Chung/ Alamy, p. 16; Rick Havner/ AP Images, pp. 16-17; Scott Cunningham/ Contributor/ Getty, p. 19 (Steve Smith Sr.); Icon Sportswire/ Contributor/ Getty, pp. 19 (Julius Peppers), 20 (mascot), 23; Cliff Hawkins/ Staff/ Getty, p. 19 (Cam Newton); DJ83JJ/ Alamy, p. 19 (Greg Olsen); Streeter Lecka/ Staff/ Getty, p. 19 (Luke Kuechly); Grindstone Media Group, p. 20 (stadium); Kevin Ruck, p. 21 (1993); Mitchell Layton/ Contributor/ Getty, p. 21 (1995); G. Newman Lowrance/ AP Images, p. 21 (2004); Jason DeCrow/ AP Images, p. 21 (2011); Zuma Press Inc./ Alamy, p. 21 (2016); Kevin C. Cox/ Staff/ Getty, p. 21 (Cam Newton).